HENRY MOORE AND LANDSCAPE
9 May – 31 August 1987

Sculpture is an art of the open-air. Daylight, sunlight is necessary to it. I would rather have a piece of my sculpture put in a landscape, almost any landscape, than in, or on, the most beautiful building I know.

Henry Moore

Cover: *King and Queen,* Bronze, 1952-3, photographed at the Yorkshire Sculpture Park by Charles Meecham

Perhaps there is something about Yorkshire itself ... Perhaps what influenced me most over wanting to do sculpture in the open air and relate my sculpture to landscape comes from my youth in Yorkshire; seeing the Yorkshire moors, seeing, I remember, a huge natural outcrop of stone (at Adel) ... and also the slag heaps which for me as a boy, as a young child, were like mountains ... Perhaps those impressions when you're young are what count.

...the slag heaps which for me as a boy, as a young child, were like mountains. They had the scale of the pyramids; they had this triangular, bare, stark quality that was just as though one were in the Alps.

owned by public galleries in London, Toronto and New York, and there is hardly a museum of modern art of importance in Europe, USA or Japan which does not own at least an example of his sculptures. Complete sets of his graphic work have been given to museums in London, Paris, Duisburg and Toronto. Few artists in the twentieth century have achieved such world-wide fame or been so generous in their support of public collections.'

Henry Moore wanted his work to be a celebration of life and nature; this is exactly what this exhibition hopes to accomplish as it is planned to celebrate the artist's great achievements and his lasting love affair with the landscape, both as a constant source of inspiration and the preferred setting for his sculpture.

It is appropriate that an exhibition dealing exclusively with Henry Moore's sculpture in the landscape should take place at the YSP, which has for the last ten years pioneered the siting, understanding and enjoyment of sculpture in the open air. When one thinks of Moore's sculpture, his statements and all that he aspired to, it is difficult, almost impossible, not to visualize large organic forms in a landscape setting. Even the hand-held works appear to have emerged from the earth and for Moore, who often thought of his sculpture as landscape, the two entities become at times almost synonymous.

INTRODUCTION

Henry Moore was born at 30 Roundhill Road, Castleford on 30 July 1898. Castleford is eight miles from the Yorkshire Sculpture Park and now forms part of the Wakefield Metropolitan District. He was the seventh of eight children and in spite of admitting to having had 'a very thin time' he remembered a loving, kindly and secure childhood and always spoke of his mother with great affection and emphasized his admiration for his father.

His father, who started life as a coal miner, was a great inspiration to all his children, encouraging them to learn and to believe in education. From this humble background Henry Moore went on to become the most eminent sculptor of this century, no other sculptor in history has had work shown so widely around the world. His fame, spanning several decades of his life, also touched many countries as John Read pointed out when he wrote the following in 1979:

'By his eightieth birthday, Henry Moore, Order of Merit, Companion of Honour, had received at least seventy-five major awards in the form of honorary degrees, memberships of art academies in several countries, and international prizes for art. He had held seventy exhibitions of his work in at least twenty-five different countries. He was the originator of some eight hundred sculptures, great and small, and more than four thousand drawings and sketches; and his more recent interest in graphics has already yielded some five hundred prints of various kinds. Major collections of his work are

HENRY MOORE AND LANDSCAPE

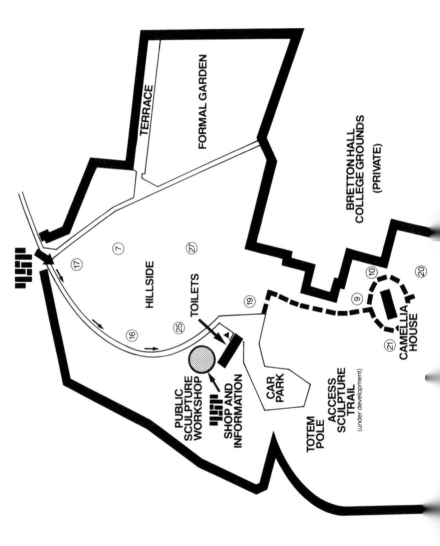

TERRACE

FORMAL GARDEN

BRETTON HALL
COLLEGE GROUNDS
(PRIVATE)

⑰

⑦

㉗

HILLSIDE

TOILETS

⑲

⑯

㉕

PUBLIC
SCULPTURE
WORKSHOP

SHOP AND
INFORMATION

CAR
PARK

TOTEM
POLE

ACCESS
SCULPTURE
TRAIL
(under development)

⑩

⑨

㉑

⑳

CAMELLIA
HOUSE

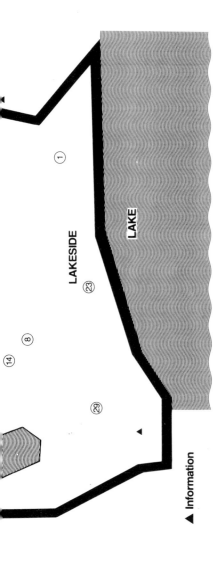

LAKESIDE

LAKE

▲ Information

Due to the large touring exhibition planned for India a number of sculptures have had to be withdrawn. However, owing to the generosity of British Gas and the support of the Henry Moore Foundation, it has been possible to retain a substantial group of sculptures until 25 October 1987.

The numbering relates to the original catalogue list

1 Large Reclining Figure 1938 Fibreglass
2 Mother and Child 1949 Bronze
7 Upright Motive No. 7 1955-6 Bronze
8 Draped Seated Woman 1957-8 Bronze
9 Seated Woman 1958-9 Bronze
10 Relief No. 1 1957 Bronze
12 Three Part Object 1960 Bronze
14 Two-Piece Reclining Figure No. 1 1961-2 Bronze
16 Three-Piece Reclining Figure No. 1 1961-2 Bronze
17 The Arch 1963-9 Fibreglass

18 Three-Piece Reclining Figure No. 2: Bridge Prop 1961 Bronze
19 Locking Piece 1963-9 Fibreglass
20 Knife Edge Two-Piece 1962-5 Bronze
21 Large Totem Head 1968 Bronze
23 Oval and Points 1968-70 Bronze
24 Two-Piece Reclining Figure: Points 1967-70 Bronze
25 Reclining Figure 1969-70 Bronze
27 Hill Arches 1973 Bronze
29 Three-Piece Reclining Figure: Draped 1975 Bronze

YORKSHIRE SCULPTURE PARK

BRETTON HALL · WEST BRETTON · WAKEFIELD · WF4 4LG

Although he was always interested in outdoor sculpture the true potential of the placement of sculpture in the landscape only became fully apparent after the siting of his sculptures in the Keswick estate in Dumfrieshire. *King and Queen* (catalogue no. 6), *Standing Figure* (catalogue no. 3), *Two Piece Reclining Figure* and *Glenkiln Cross* all placed majestically and spaciously in the Scottish landscape prompted Moore to state '...seeing them has convinced me that sculpture – at any rate my sculpture is seen best in this way and not in a Museum.'

Throughout his life landscape and natural forms were, for Henry Moore, great sources of energy and inspiration. '...spaces, distance, landscape, plants, pebbles, rocks, bones, all excite me and give me ideas.' Rarely did he draw or work directly from nature, preferring to store up the visual data and then, at a later stage, to draw, 'not copying', but creating from his imagination,

transcribing his visual experiences into a rich vocabulary, which expressed his love and concern for nature. Nature, he said, provided an inexhaustible stimulus. Constant looking was essential, as it was important for vision to be '...renewed and refreshed' for '...an artist's raw material is what he has seen and done.' Even at the age of eighty-seven, and in failing health, Moore still felt the urge to go into the landscape daily. '...I enjoy my afternoon drives. I see different things, even if I go the same route, because the light is always different.' He maintained that through his work he was attempting to add to people's understanding of life and nature, helping them to open their eyes and be more sensitive.

For Moore, the production of art '...can only come by the development and experience of a lifetime.' This concept, relying upon the assimilation of diverse perceptual experiences, is embodied within the three main themes

running throughout his work: *Mother and Child; The Reclining Figure;* and *Interior and Exterior Forms.* When developing the *Reclining Figures* he began to appreciate the potential of relating figures to landscape and he combined rock and mountain forms with the human figure in two and three piece sculptures.

His earliest recollection of landscape was in Yorkshire, and he frequently acknowledged the influence of the landscape of his childhood. This environment provided a stark contrast between the enclosed back streets of Castleford and the openness of the surrounding Yorkshire countryside.

It was at school that Moore became involved in art and he saw his first real sculptures at Methley church, just outside Castleford. He loved school, gaining great pleasure from the drawing lessons at elementary school and often he paid tribute to the encouragement of Alice Gostick, his art teacher at Castleford Secondary School. After the First World War he attended the Leeds College of Art and in 1921 he won a scholarship to study at the Royal College of Art in London. Seven years later he held his first one person exhibition. Herbert Read, who was to become a close friend and supporter, wrote a favourable review in The Listener. Moore was also encouraged by the purchase of drawings by Augustus John and Jacob Epstein. The catalogue for Moore's next exhibition had an introduction by Epstein who made the prophetic remark '...for the future of sculpture in England Henry Moore is vitally important.' Despite this impressive support there was also opposition, as one critic wrote, '...the cult of ugliness thrives at the hand of Mr Moore.' There was also a move to have him dismissed from his part-time teaching post at the Royal College of Art which, at that time, was his only form of income. The old students' association supported this move by passing a resolution demanding his dismissal as a tutor. He was accused of being a 'corrupter of youth', 'a Bolshevik' and 'a man who had been feeding on garbage.'

My first serious bit of wood carving was the school memorial for former students wounded or killed in the First World War.

In 1929 he married Irina Radetsky, who was a great source of inspiration and remained his 'most valuable critic.' Throughout his life he never compromised his ideals in the face of public derision nor for financial reasons. In spite of his enormous success later in life, his life-style hardly changed and up until the age of eighty-five he worked seven days a week.

Although very conscious of his working class origins, Moore, according to Stephen Spender, never felt socially inferior or superior to anyone and '...fitted into every society simply as a member of the human race.' The late Kenneth Clark once remarked to Spender '...that if a race inhabiting a distant planet were discovered and it was necessary to send them a representative of humanity, no better ambassador could be chosen than Henry Moore.'

Although this exhibition concentrates on the *plein-air,* reference must be made to Henry Moore's graphic work. The sketch books provide a fascinating record and offer insight into his working methods. His two-dimensional work can be very powerful and has left some haunting and evocative images, most notably the shelter drawings. These drawings, of people sheltering in the London Underground during the blitz, have become one of the most indelible visual reports on war in the history of art.

Later in the War, in 1942, Moore visited Castleford to do a series of drawings at Wheldale Colliery where his father had worked. He had never been down a mine before and the experience was overwhelming.

'Crawling on sore hands and knees and reaching the actual coal-face was the biggest experience. If one were asked to describe what hell might be like, this would do. A dense darkness you could touch, the whirring din of the coal-cutting machine, throwing into the air black dust so thick that the light beams from the miners' lamps could only shine into it a few inches – the impression of numberless short pit-props placed only a foot or two apart, to support above them a mile's weight of rock and earth ceiling – all this in the stifling heat. I have never had a tougher day in my life, of physical effort and exertion – but I wanted to show the Deputy that I could stand just as much as the miners.'

During the Second World War Henry Moore's London studio was bombed and so he and his wife, Irina, moved to a house in Perry Green, near to Much Hadham in Hertfordshire where their daughter, Mary, was born in 1946. Up until 1950 his studio was still a small building adjoining the house. Since then, as P J Kavanagh has pointed out in a recent article 'without in any sense wooing a public, or making concessions to it...' Henry Moore has become '...the world's favourite contemporary sculptor.' With greater international success and recognition the operation at Perry Green has grown and there are now several studios, a sculpture garden and the Henry Moore Foundation.

Henry Moore's great success has meant that many of his major outdoor sculptures are permanently sited or belong to galleries in other countries. For this reason there are a number of omissions. However this exhibition includes work produced between the period 1938 and 1983 and all the sculptures were conceived with the landscape or open air in mind.

The exhibition demonstrates how Henry Moore's imaginative powers developed over the years and how he expanded his ideas to meet the challenge of working on a massive scale producing sculpture which becomes its own architecture, of which The Arch (catalogue no. 17) is a good example. Standing fifteen feet in height it can be seen here in fibreglass. There is also a version carved in Travertine marble and permanently sited in Kensington Gardens in London. Moore always thought that bronze was a wonderful material for the open air as it weathers and lasts in all climates and is more impervious than stone. He had, on the other hand, no reservations about solving practical problems by using fibreglass which he considered to be an acceptable substitute for other materials.

In his book, Henry Moore: Sculptures in Landscape, Stephen Spender suggested that Moore was staking out a claim for parts of the countryside but also for the future and he went on to ponder how his sculptures '...will look in fifty or a hundred years time, on hills, on plains, in woodlands, among vegetation, against the fool-proof sky, in rain, against the sea, in the changing light, changing in appearance every minute. If they are not vandalized by the orgiastic Dionysians of our time – the age of terrorists and druggists – or destroyed in nuclear war – they may seem survivals from a great age of art at once individualist and of the liberated unconscious of the beginning of the twentieth century.'

Henry Moore's lucid, thoughtful and clearly articulated statements relating to his sculpture, ideas and life have previously been well documented (see page 51). Throughout the catalogue a number of selected statements by the artist have been used to provide a greater insight into his development and work and, in particular, to emphasize his love of landscape and of placing sculpture in the open air. John Hedgecoe, who over a period of thirty years had many conversations with the artist, said that '...nothing he ever says is for effect or to impress and he always thinks ahead about what he is going to say.'

The artists that Henry Moore admired most had, he felt, a life-giving power in their work that extended belief and understanding beyond normal perception. This vital force can also be found in Moore's own work. It transcends national barriers and its universal imagery touches the collective unconscious creating international understanding and goodwill.

Henry Moore often said that sculpture gained by finding a setting which suits its mood and that when this happened there was great gain for the sculpture and the setting. I hope that we have found many such settings.

Henry Moore died at Perry Green on 31 August 1986. This home-coming in the Yorkshire landscape, so near to his roots, seems to complete his spiritual journey. We are privileged to mount this exhibition in honour of our founding Patron; a magnificent artist and a great ambassador for the human race.

PETER MURRAY

HENRY MOORE

The long and productive career of Henry Moore provides the key to understanding the development of British sculpture in this century. Like Picasso, Moore has given us a standard by which to judge the achievements of each decade from the 1920s.

The years leading up to the 1914-18 War are characterized by a search for an alternative language of form to replace the Hellenistic mode which had dominated post-Renaissance sculpture. Primitive art – meaning the art of cultures outside of western tradition, but including an interest in medieval art, folk art and pre-history – provided that alternative. Like Picasso and his circle in Paris, Epstein and Gaudier Brzeska shocked a somnolent world into varied conditions of anger and incredulity by the vitality and originality of their work. Henry Moore has recorded his gratitude to Epstein for taking the 'brick-bats', but his own early interest in primitive art and abstraction fanned the embers of that conflagration, and there is little evidence of widespread public acceptance of Henry Moore's work until after the Second World War when his stature as the leading sculptor of the twentieth century was beyond reasonable doubt.

Since the War Henry Moore has become a household name far beyond this country. He is the most written about and discussed sculptor of all time. The development of still photography and film has meant that his work is documented in unprecedented detail. The growth of publishing, particularly magazines and catalogues, fed by this explosion of photographic imagery, has circulated images of Moore's sculptures throughout the world. In his widespread commissions, and the extent to which his work has been exhibited and collected around the world, he is unique.

Despite the super-human implications of this process, Henry Moore remained emphatically a human being, a sculptor of humanity. There are people who, in explanation of this phenomenon, would point out that he was a Yorkshireman. What is without doubt is that the landscape of Yorkshire exerted a powerful and lasting influence upon his sculpture. Moore found ideas for sculpture in nature – a leaf or pebble; bone, rock formation or the sweeping movement of a range of hills punctuated by valleys and hollows – the variety of shape, seasonal colour and texture enlivened by a changing light under the broad Yorkshire sky.

To many people the reclining figure is the essential subject for Moore's sculpture. From the mid 1920s he returned again and again to this theme which came to represent the most profound statements about humanity, and which ultimately fused mankind and landscape within a pantheistic atmosphere. In so doing, the specific meaning, whether secular or religious, and the particular gender and style became submerged. Like all great and timeless art the reclining figure expressed a mystery which spoke to something within us which was too deep and old for our contemporary consciousness to fully grasp, identify and categorize. The resulting sculpture communicates a wholeness and completeness which is not simply a result of the, often complex, formal relationships within the sculpture but is a response to the poetic and spiritual depth of the work.

This achievement becomes still more remarkable when we recall the opposing points of departure for the theme of the reclining figure in Moore's work. For example, the primitive Mayan votive image of the Rain God, Chacmool, and the idealized naturalism of the reclining male figure, Illissus, from the Parthenon. Moore synthesizes where other artists would choose between them. This triumphant synthesis of two polarities of art places Moore's work on a level with the greatest artists of the past.

The *Earth Mother* interpretation of many of Moore's reclining figures can be helpful for its poetic and mysterious connotations, but, as a generalized concept, it should not obscure the individuality of each sculpture. We are conscious of the inner life, the weight and strength of limbs and the implied movement of the body. The figures are more often alert than in repose, and their abstract heads contemplate an horizon beyond our vision.

As a subject, the reclining figure is quintessentially sculptural. It offers stability with freedom in the treatment of the mass which, unlike the standing figure, is not required to balance upon two slender uprights.

Despite lively examples from Greek and Etruscan art the reclining figure has, since the Renaissance, been a subject more often for painters than sculptors. Its association with monumental art began to be displaced by Rodin and Maillol in the latter part of the nineteenth century and the reclining figure became a popular subject with the cubist sculptors in France. But, their solutions owed more to painting than to sculpture, and it was left to Henry Moore to demonstrate the vitality and potential for expression within the traditional theme of the reclining figure.

This exhibition at the Yorkshire Sculpture Park provides a unique opportunity to see and experience Moore's sculpture within his own landscape. The eighteenth century layout of the Park is itself a fusion of art and nature which provides a rich variety of setting and mood. From the architecture of the terracing in the formal gardens, to the flowing expanse of open landscape towards the lakes, there are variations of vista and enclosure enlivened by ground which rises and falls in a rhythmic movement. It is already apparent that the description of the landscape has more than a superficial application to the sculpture within it.

Anyone who had the good fortune to compare Moore's sculptures displayed in Florence in 1972, and in Bradford in 1978, would surely agree that the quality of the shifting light of Yorkshire overcame the limitations of Bradford as a setting and background when compared to the beauty of Florence and the Forte di Belvedere. The combination of this pure light and the superb landscape at the Yorkshire Sculpture Park is, I believe, unequalled.

ROBERT HOPPER

I have always enjoyed landscape
and responded to a natural, outdoor
environment, rocks and hills, the
shape of the earth, the sight of trees
and clouds and sky. I like my large
sculptures to be outdoors, in
landscape.

1 Large Reclining Figure 1983 Fibreglass

2   Mother and Child 1949 Bronze

In theory, the double figure with its greater bulk should be more effective in an open setting than the single figure, but the extreme openness of the Scottish setting for the single figure has upset whatever preconceptions I had. In the bleak and lonely setting of a grouse moor the figure itself becomes an image of loneliness, and on its outcrop of rock, its lean, skeletonic forms stand out sharp and clear against the sky, looking as if stripped to the bone by the winds of several centuries.

3   Standing Figure 1950 Fibreglass

The *Festival Reclining Figure* is perhaps my first sculpture where the space and the form are completely dependent on and inseparable from each other. I had reached the stage where I wanted my sculpture to be truly three-dimensional. In my earliest use of holes in sculpture, the holes were features in themselves. Now the space and the form are so naturally fused that they are one.

4   Reclining Figure: Festival 1951 Bronze

I became absorbed by the problems of the draped figure...Drapery played a very important part in the shelter drawings I made in 1940 and 1941 and what I began to learn then about its function as form gave me the intention to use drapery in sculpture in a more realistic way...And my first visit to Greece in 1951 perhaps helped to strengthen this intention...Drapery can emphasize the tension in a figure...drapery can also by its direction over the form make more obvious the section, that is show shape. It need not be just a decorative addition, but can serve to stress the sculptural idea of the figure.

Also in my mind was to connect the contrast of the size of the folds, here small, fine and delicate, in other places big and heavy, with the form of mountains, which are the crinkled skin of the earth.

5   Draped Reclining Figure 1952-3 Bronze

Perhaps the 'clue' to the group is the King's head, which is a combination of a crown, beard and face, symbolising a mixture of primitive kingship and a kind of animal, Pan-like quality. The King is more relaxed and assured in pose than the Queen, who is more upright and consciously queenly. When I came to do the hands and feet of the figures, they gave me a chance to express my ideas further by making them more realistic – to bring out the contrast between human grace and the concept of power in primitive kingship.

6 King and Queen 1952-3 Bronze

7   Upright Motive No. 7
1955-6 Bronze

Sculpture should always at first sight have some obscurities and further meanings. People should want to go on looking and thinking; it should never tell all about itself immediately. Initially both sculpture and painting must need effort to be fully appreciated, or else it is just an empty immediacy like a poster, which is designed to be read by the people on top of a bus in half a second. In fact all art should have some more mystery and meaning to it than is apparent to a quick observer.

10   Relief No. 1 1959 Bronze

8   Draped Seated Woman 1957-8 Bronze

Once a figure is in two pieces you don't expect it to be realistic, and therefore its relationship or analogy to landscape seems to be more natural. Again – with a single piece of sculpture, it is easier to guess what it is to be like from the other side; but when it is in two pieces, there are bigger surprises when you go round it, because one part will overlap another one and going round it becomes like a journey, as you have a different view all the time.

11 Two-Piece Reclining Figure No. 2 1960 Bronze

Three-Part Object is a strange work, even for me. Three similar forms are balanced at angles to each other. In my mind it has a connection with insect life, possibly centipedes. Each segment has a leg, and there is an element in the sculpture nearer to an animal organism than a human one.

12 Three-Part Object 1960 Bronze

13 Seated Woman: Thin Neck 1961 Bronze

In this figure the thin neck and head, though by contrast with the width and bulk of the body, gives more monumentality to the work.

If it form the one landscape which we, the inconstant ones
    Are constantly homesick for, this is chiefly
Because it dissolves in water. Mark these rounded slopes
    With their surface fragrance of thyme, and, beneath,
A secret system of caves and conduits, hear the springs
    That spurt out everywhere with a chuckle,
Each filling a private pool for its fish and carving
    Its own little ravine whose cliffs entertain
The butterfly and the lizard.

In Praise of a Limestone by W H Auden.

14 Two-Piece Reclining Figure No. 3
    1961 Bronze

This sculpture has been called *Standing Figure – Knife-Edge* also *Standing Figure – Bone* and again, *Winged Figure*. All three titles have some relevance to what it is, and how it came about.

Since my student days I have liked the shape of bones, and have drawn them, studied them in the Natural History Museum, found them on seashores and saved them out of the stewpot.

There are many structural and sculptural principles to be learnt from bones, e.g. that in spite of their lightness they have great strength. Some bones, such as the breast bones of birds, have the lightweight fineness of a knife-blade. Finding such a bone led to me using this knife-edge thinness in 1961 in a sculpture *Seated Woman: Thin Neck* catalogue no. 13, illustrated page 22. Later in 1961 I used this knife-edged thinness throughout a whole figure, and produced this *Standing Figure*.

Sculpture has some disadvantages compared with painting, but it can have one great advantage over painting – that it can be looked at from all round; and if this attitude is used and fully exploited then it can give to sculpture a continual, changing, never-ending surprise and interest.

In walking round this sculpture the width and flatness from the front gradually change through the three-quarter views into the thin sharp edges of the side views, and then back again to the width seen from the back.

And the top half of the figure bends backwards, is angled towards the sky, opens itself to the light in a rising upward movement – and this may be why, at one time, I called it *Winged Figure*.

In a sculptor's work all sorts of past experiences and influences are fused and used – and somewhere in this work there is a connection with the so-called *Victory of Samothrace* in the Louvre – and I would like to think that others see something Greek in this *Standing Figure*.

15 Large Standing Figure:
Knife Edge 1976 Bronze

I realised what an advantage a separated two-piece composition could have in relating figures to landscape. Knees and breasts are mountains. Once these two parts become separated you don't expect it to be a naturalistic figure; therefore, you can justifiably make it like a landscape or a rock. If it is in a single figure, you can guess what it's going to be like. If it is in two pieces, there's a bigger surprise, you have more unexpected views; therefore the special advantage over painting – of having the possibility of many different views – is more fully exploited.

The front view doesn't enable one to foresee the back view. As you move round it, the two parts overlap or they open up and there's space between. Sculpture is like a journey. You have a different view as you return. The three-dimensional world is full of surprises in a way that a two-dimensional world could never be...

16 Three-Piece Reclining Figure No. 1 1961-2 Bronze

Now in ordinary daylight – particularly English daylight, English weather, which can be very diffused and very even – only a sculpture which really has completely realised form will tell at all. Incised relief, or surface scratchings won't show in dull English weather. Only your big architectural contrasts of masses – real sculptural power, real sculptural organisation – will tell at all on a dull day. Therefore if one gets used to working out-of-doors, to be satisfied with it one will be challenged into making sculpture that has some reality to it – like the reality of nature around it.

17 The Arch 1963-9 Fibreglass

18 Three-Piece Reclining Figure No. 2: Bridge Prop 1961 Bronze

19   Locking Piece 1963-9

Locking-Piece came about from two pebbles which I was playing with and which seemed to fit each other and lock together, and this gave me the idea of making a two-piece sculpture – not that the forms weren't separate, but that they knitted together. I did several little plaster maquettes, and eventually one, nearest to the shape this big one is now, pleased me the most and then I began making the big one.

21 Large Totem Head 1968 Bronze

Out of doors in England the light is as good for sculpture as anybody could want. You have to make strong forms that really exist because they are not for ever flattered or exaggerated by sunlight.

20   Knife Edge Two-Piece 1962-5 Bronze

23 Oval and Points 1968-70 Bronze

22 Upright Motive No. 9 1979 Bronze

Bronze is a wonderful material, it weathers and lasts in all climates. One only has to look at the ancient bronzes, for example, the Marcus Aurelius equestrian statue in Rome. I love to stand beneath this statue, because it is so big. Under the belly of the horse, the rain has left marks which emphasize the section where it has run down over the centuries. This statue is nearly two thousand years old, yet the bronze is in perfect condition. Bronze is really more impervious to the weather than most stone.

24 Two-Piece Reclining Figure: Points 1969-70 Bronze

...I like seeing sculpture in relation to nature, and have done ever since I can remember doing sculpture. Now I have had the chance to make the kind of studio where one can switch from indoor to outdoor easily, and even in bad weather now I can work out-of-doors and be under cover... ...

25   Reclining Figure 1969-70 Bronze

26 Reclining Connected Forms 1969 Bronze

The idea of one form inside another form may owe some of its incipient beginnings to my interest at one stage when I discovered armour. I spent many hours in the Wallace Collection, in London, looking at armoury.

Now armour is an outside shell like the shell of a snail which is there to protect the more vulnerable forms inside, as it is in human armour which is hard and put on to protect the soft body. This has led sometimes to the idea of the *Mother and Child* when the outer form, the mother, is protecting the inner form, the child, like a mother does protect her child.

27 Hill Arches 1973 Bronze

28 Goslar Warrior 1973-4 Bronze

The sky is one of the things I like most about 'sculpture with nature'. There is no background to sculpture better than the sky, because you are contrasting solid form with its opposite – space. The sculpture then has no competition, no distraction from other solid objects. If I wanted the most fool-proof of backgrounds for a sculpture I would always choose the sky.

29 Three-Piece Reclining Figure:
Draped 1975 Bronze

30 Reclining Figure: Angles 1979 Bronze

31 Reclining Figure: Hand 1978-9 Bronze

32 Draped Reclining Mother and Baby 1983 Bronze

33 Mother and Child on Block Seat 1983 Bronze

LIST OF WORKS

LH followed by a number is the reference given in the complete catalogue raisonné of sculpture included in the volumes on Henry Moore published by Lund Humphries & Co Ltd, London and Bradford.

1 Large Reclining Figure 1938 (cast 1983)
L 1036 cm approximately
Fibreglass
LH 192B
The Henry Moore Foundation
There is an edition of two casts in bronze (one at the Henry Moore Foundation) which were based on an earlier sculpture cast in lead measuring 33cm long, now in the Museum of Modern Art, New York

2 Mother and Child 1949
H 81 cm
Bronze, unique cast
LH 269B
The Henry Moore Foundation
This sculpture relates to *Family Group* 1945-49 commissioned for Barclay School, Stevenage, Herts, another cast being in the Tate Gallery, London

3 Standing Figure 1950
H 221 cm
Fibreglass
LH 290
The Henry Moore Foundation
The first cast in bronze of this figure was placed in the landscape at Glenkiln, Shawhead, Dumfrieshire.

4 Reclining Figure: Festival 1951
L 228.5 cm
Bronze, edition of 5
LH 292
Scottish National Gallery of Modern Art, Edinburgh
This is the cast commissioned by the Arts Council of Great Britain for the 1951 Festival of Britain exhibition in London

5 Draped Reclining Figure 1952-3
L 157.5 cm
Bronze, edition of 3
LH 336
The Henry Moore Foundation

6 King and Queen 1952-3
H 164 cm
Bronze, edition of 6
LH 350
The Henry Moore Foundation
Originally commissioned for the Open Air Sculpture Park at Middelheim near Antwerp in Belgium. Another cast is placed in the landscape at Glenkiln, Shawhead, Dumfrieshire.

7 Upright Motive No. 7 1955-6
H 163.8 cm
Bronze, edition of 6
LH 386
The Henry Moore Foundation

8 Draped Seated Woman 1957-8
H 185.5 cm
Bronze, edition of 6
LH 428
Stifford Estate, Stepney, Tower Hamlets, London

9 Seated Woman 1958-9 (cast 1975)
H 190.5 cm
Bronze, edition of 6
LH 440
The Henry Moore Foundation

10 Relief No. 1 1959
H 223.5 cm
Bronze, edition of 6
LH 450
The Henry Moore Foundation

11 Two-Piece Reclining Figure No. 2 1960
L 259 cm
Bronze, edition of 7
LH 458
The Henry Moore Foundation
One cast is placed outside the Scottish National Gallery of Modern Art, Edinburgh

12 Three-Part Object 1960
H 123.5 cm
Bronze, edition of 9
LH 470
The Henry Moore Foundation

13 Seated Woman: Thin Neck 1961
H 162.5 cm
Bronze, edition of 7
LH 472
Laing Art Gallery, Newcastle upon Tyne, Tyne and Wear

14 Two-Piece Reclining Figure No. 3 1961
L 239 cm
Bronze, edition of 7
LH 478
Brandon Estate, London Borough of Southwark

15 Large Standing Figure: Knife Edge 1976
H 358.2 cm
Bronze, edition of 6
LH 482A
The Henry Moore Foundation
One cast is in Greenwich Park, London

16 Three-Piece Reclining Figure No. 1 1961-2
L 287 cm
Bronze, edition of 7
LH 500
Tate Gallery, London

17 The Arch 1963-9
H 610 cm
Fibreglass
LH 503B
The Henry Moore Foundation
A carving of this sculpture in Travertine marble was donated by the artist to the Department of Environment for a permanent site overlooking the Serpentine in Kensington Gardens, London

**18 Three-Piece Reclining Figure No.2:
Bridge Prop** 1961
L 251.5 cm
Bronze, edition of 6
LH 513
City Art Gallery, Leeds

19 Locking Piece 1963-9
H 292 cm
Fibreglass
LH 515
The Henry Moore Foundation
One of the edition of three bronzes, given
by the artist to the Tate Gallery, is now
permanently sited on Millbank near Vauxhall
Bridge overlooking the Thames.

20 Knife Edge Two-Piece 1962-5
L 366 cm
Bronze, edition of 3
LH 516
The Henry Moore Foundation
The cast purchased by the Contemporary
Art Society is now sited near Parliament
Square opposite the House of Lords

21 Large Totem Head 1968
H 344 cm
Bronze, edition of 8
LH 577
Tate Gallery, London

22 Upright Motive No. 9 1979
H 332 cm
Bronze, edition of 6
LH 586A
The Henry Moore Foundation
One cast is at present on loan to York
Minster

23 Oval with Points 1968-70
H 332 cm
Bronze
LH 596
The Henry Moore Foundation

24 Two-Piece Reclining Figure: Points
1969-70
L 365 cm approximately
Bronze, edition of 7
LH 606
The Henry Moore Foundation

25 Reclining Figure 1969-70
L 343 cm
Bronze, edition of 6
LH 608
The Henry Moore Foundation

26 Reclining Connected Forms 1969
L 213 cm
Bronze, edition of 9
LH 612
The Henry Moore Foundation

27 Hill Arches 1973
L 550 cm approximately
Bronze, edition of 3
LH 636
The Henry Moore Foundation

28 Goslar Warrior 1973-4
L 249 cm
Bronze, edition of 7
LH 641
The Henry Moore Foundation
Derives its title from the City of Goslar in West
Germany which was the purchaser of the
first cast. There were two earlier sculptures
on this theme: *Warrior with Shield* 1953-4
belonging to the Birmingham City Art
Gallery and *Falling Warrior* 1956-7 in the
collections of the Walker Art Gallery,
Liverpool and the Huddersfield Art Gallery

**29 Three-Piece Reclining Figure:
Draped** 1975
L 447 cm
Bronze, edition of 7
LH 655
The Henry Moore Foundation

30 Reclining Figure: Angles 1979
L 218.4 cm
Bronze, edition of 9
LH 675
The Henry Moore Foundation

31 Reclining Figure: Hand 1978-9
L 221 cm
Bronze, edition of 9
LH 709
The Henry Moore Foundation

32 Draped Reclining Mother and Baby
1983
L 265.4 cm
Bronze, edition of 9
LH 822
The Henry Moore Foundation

33 Mother and Child on Block Seat 1983
H 244 cm
Bronze, edition of 9
LH 838
The Henry Moore Foundation

The fibreglass sculptures were made
specifically for exhibitions when it was not
possible to obtain the originals.

BIOGRAPHY

1898 Born 30 July at 30 Roundhill Road, Castleford, Yorkshire, the seventh of eight children. His father was a miner, both parents coming originally from Lincolnshire.

1909 The family moves from 30 Roundhill Road (demolished in 1974) to 56 Smawthorne Lane in Castleford. When attending Sunday School he hears a story about Michelangelo and thinks about being a sculptor.

1910 Obtains a scholarship while at Temple Street Elementary School (now Castleford Half Acres First School) to the Grammar School (now the Comprehensive). Here he meets with encouragement from the headmaster and in particular from the Art Mistress, Alice Gostick, who helps develop his talents in drawing and sculpture and who lends him copies of The Studio magazine. She also arranges for some of her pupils to attend evening classes in pottery and for Clokie's (the local pottery firm) to allow their pots to be fired.

During childhood, on visits to his aunt at Methley, he sees the alabaster carvings in St Oswald's Church, although it is the Gothic carvings on the capitals and gorbels he draws and which make a lasting impression. Excursions from school and with his father are also made to local beauty spots such as Adel Rock.

1915 Enrols at Teacher Training College on his father's advice (three of the family have already become teachers). Starts as a student-teacher although already wishing to be a sculptor.

1916 Travels to London to volunteer for the Civil Service Rifles of the 19th London Regiment. For the first time visits the National Gallery and the British Museum.

1917 Enlists in February as a private and in the summer is sent to France on active service. Gassed in the Battle of Cambrai he is sent back to hospital in England.

1918 Becomes a PT Instructor but is redrafted to France just before The Armistice.

1919 After demobilisation returns to teaching in Castleford. Successful in obtaining an ex-service-man's grant he enters Leeds College of Art in September. Barbara Hepworth, the sculptor, and Raymond Coxon, the painter, are among his contemporaries.

1919-21 During this time makes several visits to the home of the Vice-Chancellor of Leeds University, Sir Michael Sadler, to study his collection of African sculpture and Impressionist paintings. Although still living at Castleford he spends many evenings reading in Leeds Reference Library where he discovers a book, Vision and Design by Roger Fry, which is to influence him.

1921 Wins a Royal Exhibition Scholarship in Sculpture of £90 a year and in September enters the Royal College of Art in London where he is to study modelling and drawing. For the next three years spends many hours in the British Museum studying antique and primitive sculpture but especially Mexican sculpture.

1922 Carves in his free time and draws constantly. Starts a series of sculpture on the theme of *Mother and Child*.

1923 Pays first of regular visits to Paris. (He is later to meet Picasso and Zadkine and in 1945 Brancusi).

1924 Graduates from the Royal College of Art and is appointed as Instructor in the Sculpture School for a term of seven years to teach two days a week. His carvings include his first reclining figure.

1925 Visits France and Italy following the award the previous year of the Royal College of Art Travelling Scholarship. Spends some time in Florence but in six months also visits Rome, Pisa, Siena, Assisi, Padua, Ravenna and Venice. Is particularly impressed by the works of Giotto, Masaccio, the Pisani and Michelangelo and also by Etruscan sculpture.

1926 Work included for the first time in a group exhibition in London.

1927 Continues to carve in wood and stone but also explores the use of concrete and terracotta.

1928 First one-man exhibition in London held at the Warren Gallery. The art critic of the The Morning Post demands his dismissal from the Royal College of Art. However, Jacob Epstein buys several sculptures and the Whitworth Art Gallery, University of Manchester, acquires two drawings. Also receives his first commission, a relief carving 'The West Wind' (244 cm long) for the facade of the new Underground building at St James's, London.

1929 Marries Irina Radetsky, a student in the Royal College of Art Painting School. They live in Hampstead. Near neighbours are Barbara Hepworth, Ben Nicholson, Winifred Nicholson and later Gabo and Mondrian.

1930 The first full-length article on his work is published in Apollo Magazine. Elected to the 7 & 5 Society, a group of avant-garde artists who arrange their own exhibitions.

1931 The Director of the Hamburg Kunsthalle buys a sculpture and several drawings from an exhibition in London at the Leicester Galleries, where he is to exhibit regularly for many years.

1932 Leaves the Royal College of Art on appointment as Head of the new Department of Sculpture at Chelsea School of Art.

1933 Elected to Unit One, he contributes to the group's magazine.

1934 Henry Moore Sculptor by Herbert Read, the poet and art critic, who was also born in Yorkshire, is published by Zwemmers. Buys a small house at Kingston near Canterbury which enables him to work outside on carvings in the vacations. Creates two and three piece compositions.

1936 Represented in the International Surrealist Exhibition in London which includes work by Dali, Ernst and Miro. Through the intermediary of Sir Michael Sadler, sells his first sculpture to a public gallery in the USA, the Museum of Modern Art in New York. Carves *Reclining Figure* in elmwood which is acquired in 1942 by Wakefield City Art Gallery.

1937 Works on a series of stringed figures. Casts sculptures in lead.

1938 Takes part in abstract art exhibition at the Stedelijk Museum in Amsterdam, the first time he exhibits abroad.

1939 Gives up teaching to devote all his time to sculpture and drawing. *Recumbent Figure* 1938 in Hornton stone (140 cms long) is presented to the Tate Gallery by the Contemporary Art Society.

1940 Returns to London and sketches air raid scenes and studies of people sheltering in the London Underground. Appointed official War Artist 1940-42 to carry out his shelter drawings which were later presented to several regional art galleries. After his Hampstead studio is damaged by bombs, he moves to Hoglands, a seventeenth century farmhouse in Hertfordshire, where he is to live for the rest of his life.

1941 The first retrospective exhibition (36 sculptures and 69 drawings) is organized at Temple Newsam House, Leeds, by Philip Hendy, later Director of the National Gallery. *Reclining Figure* 1929 in Hornton stone is acquired by Leeds City Art Gallery.

1942 Accepts a second commission from the War Artists Advisory Committee, this time to record miners at work. He chooses to spend two weeks at Wheldale Colliery drawing men working at the coalface. (These studies may have influenced the modelling of the male figures in the family groups of the next few years and in *King and Queen*).

1943 Accepts a commission to carve a *Madonna and Child* for St Matthew's Church in Northampton. One of several studies was later used for the *Claydon Madonna and Child* 1948-9 (122cm high) now at St Mary's Church, Barham in Suffolk. The first of his many one-man exhibitions is held in the USA at the Buccholz Gallery in New York.

1944-47 Makes several studies of family groups, the larger of these being for Barclay School, Stevenage and for Harlow New Town.

1945 Created Honorary Doctor of Literature at the University of Leeds, his first academic award. (He was to receive honours and awards from nearly all European countries and from many American universities). Now has his sculptures cast in bronze. This is to give him greater freedom in modelling.

1947-48 From a small model made in 1945 he carves *Three Standing Figures* (214 cm high) in stone quarried at Darley Dale in Derbyshire. This group is purchased by the Contemporary Art Society for a site in Battersea Park in London, where it has remained.

1948 Invited to show his sculptures and drawings in the British Pavilion at the Venice Biennale (with paintings by Turner in the main rooms) he receives the International Sculpture Prize. Many requests for exhibitions are now received from foreign museums and galleries.

1949 An exhibition of 53 sculptures and 23 drawings at the Wakefield City Art Gallery.

1949-50 An exhibition of sculptures and drawings is toured by the British Council to the major public galleries of Brussels, Paris, Amsterdam, Hamburg, Dusseldorf and Berne. (The British Council is to tour major exhibitions of his work abroad almost continuously from 1950 onwards).

1951 First major retrospective in London at the Tate Gallery. Travels widely in Greece and on return experiments with drapery in figures. First film made for the BBC by John Read. Over the next 35 years his work is to be acquired by nearly all the major public collections in the world.

1952-53 Carves a screen (305 cm high and 808 cm long) for the facade of the Time Life Building in New Bond Street, London and completes *Draped Reclining Figure* commissioned for the terrace of the same building. The City of Antwerp commissions *King and Queen* for the Open Air Museum at Middelheim Park.

1953 Awarded the International Prize for Sculpture at the 2nd Sao Paulo Biennale. Visits Brazil and Mexico.

1955 Made a Companion of Honour by Her Majesty The Queen. Becomes a Trustee of the National Gallery having previously served fourteen years on the Board of the Tate Gallery.

1956 Invited to execute a sculpture for the outside of the new Unesco Building in Paris. His first ideas are for work in bronze but decides finally to execute a reclining figure in Travertine marble.

1957 Spends time in Italy near Carrara carving the Unesco figure (498 cm long). The working model in bronze is now at the Tate Gallery.

1959 Participates in the 5th Tokyo Biennale of Art and is given the Foreign Minister's Award. Begins the series of two piece reclining figures.

1960 Retrospective exhibition at the Whitechapel Art Gallery, London.

1962 Made Honorary Freeman of the Borough of Castleford 'in recognition and appreciation of the great contribution which he has made to the enjoyment of art the world over, and to his great achievements and the world-wide fame which has attended them, remembering with particular pride and joy that he was born in Castleford, the son of a miner, and spent his early life in the town'.

1963 Received appointment to the Order of Merit.

1965 Buys small villa at Forte dei Marmi near the Carrara quarries so that he can carve there in the summer.

1966 Receives Honorary Doctorates from the Universities of York and Sheffield. Devotes time to exploring the possibilities of printmaking.

1968 His 70th birthday marked by major exhibitions at the Tate Gallery, London and the Kröller-Müller Rijksmuseum near Otterlo in Holland. Awarded the Erasmus Prize, he gives the money to help secure studios for young artists in London.

1970 Etchings based on studies of an elephant skull exhibited.

1972 Fills a sketchbook with drawings of sheep observed from his studio window. A major exhibition of his sculptures, drawings and graphics is held from May to October in and around the Forte di Belvedere overlooking Florence and is seen by over a quarter of a million people.

1974 The Henry Moore Centre opens in Toronto marking the gift of several sculptures, original plaster models and works on paper, to the Art Gallery of Ontario. Lithographs on *Stonehenge* are published by Ganymed Press with an introduction by the poet Stephen Spender.

1975 Gives talk on the BBC on the occasion of the 5th Centenary of the birth of Michelangelo.

1977 The Henry Moore Foundation is established. He gives the studios and surrounding grounds with a collection of his work to the Foundation which is also to administer grants and scholarships to art colleges in this country.

1978 His 80th birthday marked by an exhibition of over 200 drawings in London and in Toronto. Another exhibition organized by the Arts Council is held in and around the Serpentine Gallery in Hyde Park. A third is held at Cartwright Hall in Bradford. Donates 36 sculptures to the Tate Gallery. Becomes Patron of the Yorkshire Sculpture Park.

1979 Created Honorary Doctor of Letters at the University of Bradford.

1980 Presents the bronze Working Model for *Draped Reclining Figure* 1976-9 to Castleford where it is placed outside the Civic Hall.

1981 Created Honorary Freeman of the City of Leeds.

1982 The Henry Moore Gallery and the Henry Moore Centre for the Study of Sculpture open at the Leeds City Art Gallery in the presence of HM The Queen. The first exhibition is devoted to his early carvings.

1984 Created Commandeur de l'Ordre national de la Legion d'honneur by President Mitterand who visits him privately.

1986 Dies aged 88 at his home in Hertfordshire on 31 August. A Service of Thanksgiving for the Life and Work of Henry Moore is held at Westminster Abbey on 18 November.

ACKNOWLEDGEMENTS

Without the generous and perceptive sponsorship of British Gas it would not have been possible to mount this major exhibition. Their concern with the environment makes an ideal match for a project of this nature. We are grateful to the Chairman, Sir Denis Rooke CBE, FRS, FEng, and the Board of British Gas for their sponsorship of the exhibition; to Norman Blacker, Regional Chairman of British Gas North Eastern, for his initial interest in the project; also for their close interest, support and help, to Fred Plowman, Head of Public.Relations, David Butler, Information Manager (PR) and Sandra Simkins, Information Officer (PR) from British Gas headquarters in London and also to Owen O'Neill, Public Relations Manager of British Gas North Eastern.

We would like to thank the Trustees of the Henry Moore Foundation for the loan of a substantial body of work and for their financial assistance. Margaret McLeod has been encouraging since the outset and her guidance and advice has been crucial. We are also grateful for her invaluable help in compiling and preparing information for the catalogue. The staff of the Henry Moore Foundation, in Much Hadham, Hertfordshire, have shown great patience and the enthusiasm of David Mitchinson for this project was much appreciated along with the help of Ann Garrould, Betty Tinsley, Jean Askwith and Michel Muller.

On the technical side, the experience, expertise and assistance of John Farnham and Malcolm Woodward has been invaluable and is appreciated by all at the Yorkshire Sculpture Park. We are also grateful for the interest and support given by Terry Friedman from the Henry Moore Centre, Leeds.

For lending work to this exhibition we are very grateful to the Trustees of the Tate Gallery and the Trustees of the National Galleries of Scotland, The Laing Art Gallery, Newcastle upon Tyne, Leeds City Art Gallery, the Stifford Estate, Stepney, Tower Hamlets, London and the Brandon Estate, London Borough of Southwark.

We are grateful to the Museums and Galleries Commission for helping to arrange Government Indemnity and in particular to Heather Wilson for her valuable assistance.

Further funding has been gratefully received from Marks and Spencer who are sponsoring the education programme which will accompany the exhibition.

A project of this nature requires the support and dedication of many. Last, but not least, we would like to thank all those who have been associated with the project, particularly those from the Manpower Services Commission Community Project Bretton Hall College and the staff of Yorkshire Sculpture Park staff.

Robert Hopper
Chairperson, Yorkshire Sculpture Park
Management Committee
Peter Murray
Executive Director, Yorkshire Sculpture Park

In 1977 the Yorkshire Sculpture Park at Bretton Hall was opened as the first permanent Sculpture Park in Britain. Thanks to the energy and vision of the Director and his staff, coupled with the assistance of the Trustees, Management Committee and countless supporters, a great deal has been achieved in the last decade.

The unique partnership forged by the Arts Council, through Yorkshire Arts, with Wakefield Metropolitan District Council and adjacent local authorities, together with the College, has guaranteed the success of a most imaginative venture. We believe that we can still build on this dynamism and the potential of the Yorkshire Sculpture Park remains both enormous and exciting.

It is particularly fitting that the work of Henry Moore, the Yorkshire Sculpture Park's founding Patron, will be on show at a time when the Park comes of age. Clearly it gives us all very great pleasure to host such an important exhibition at a time when after only ten years the Yorkshire Sculpture Park is being seen as a centre of excellence for the art world and the community as a whole. In a small way we trust that such a landmark exhibition is a fitting tribute to a much admired artist, an Honorary Fellow of Bretton Hall College and an outstanding sculptor of international acclaim.

Dr John L Taylor
Principal, Bretton Hall.
The Lord Feversham
Chairperson, Yorkshire Sculpture Park Trustees

The quotations in the Introduction and the statements made by Henry Moore interspersed with the photographs in the catalogue were taken from the following publications:

Henry Moore on Sculpture: ed. P. James (MacDonald 1966, paper 1968/Viking 1967 & 1971).
John Hedgecoe – Henry Moore, Energy in Space: (Bruckmann 1972/NYGS 1974)
Stephen Spender – Henry Moore: Sculptures in Landscape: photographs by Geoffrey Shakerley (Studio Vista/Sterner Sens/Potter 1978)
With Henry Moore, The Artist at Work: photographed by Gemma Levine (Sidgwick & Jackson/Time Books 1978)
John Read – Henry Moore: Portrait of an Artist: (Whizzard Press/Deutsch 1979)
Henry Moore Sculpture: introduction by Franco Russoli; ed. David Mitchinson (Poligrafa/Macmillan/Rizzoli/Klett-Cotta 1981-82)
John Hedgecoe/Henry Moore – Henry Moore – My Ideas, Inspiration and Life as an Artist: (Ebury Press 1986)

A comprehensive bibliography is being prepared by the Henry Moore Foundation. It will document in detail all publications on Henry Moore from the 1920s to the present day. Information and items for inclusion should be sent to: Henry Moore Bibliography, Dane Tree House, Perry Green, Much Hadham, Hertfordshire, England.

The education programme for Henry Moore and Landscape is sponsored by Marks and Spencer.
The Yorkshire Sculpture Park is supported by the Yorkshire Arts Association, Wakefield Metropolitan District Council, Manpower Services Commission Community Programme, and the Museums and Galleries Commission.